Edward Poulson

The Wonderful Word Jah

Edward Poulson

The Wonderful Word Jah

ISBN/EAN: 9783744730471

Printed in Europe, USA, Canada, Australia, Japan

Cover: Foto ©Lupo / pixelio.de

More available books at **www.hansebooks.com**

היפלא מיהוה דבר

THE WONDERFUL WORD
"JAH."

THE CHALLENGE OF THE CHIEF RABBI REFUTED,

AND THE

ETERNAL TRINITY OF JEHOVAH EHLOHIM PROVED
FROM THE LAW AND THE PROPHETS,

WITHOUT REFERENCE TO THE NEW TESTAMENT.

THE FIRST ARTICLE REVISED AND REPRINTED FROM
"THE ROCK."

BY

EDWARD POULSON.

LONDON:
HOULSTON AND SONS, 65, PATERNOSTER ROW.
1870.

CONTENTS.

PREFACE.

THOSE readers who may not be acquainted with the Hebrew characters will have no difficulty in understanding the full sense, by a little application in following the arguments of each Section, as readily as if the Hebrew words were not inserted at all, because the corresponding interpretation is given from the Authorized Version and the Jewish translations of Isaac Leeser and Dr. Benisch.

The first article, including pages 5 to 10, appeared in the *Rock* for October 8 ,1869; but, owing to the pressure of matter upon its columns, the remaining articles could only be inserted at rather distant intervals; therefore I have condensed the series into the present pamphlet.

E. P.

FEBRUARY, 1870.

THE WONDERFUL WORD "JAH."

ה' אלהינו ה' אהד—DEUT. vi. 4.

---◆---

SECTION I.

AT the synod of the Jewish Rabbis recently held, the three
following new principles were recognized: 1. Individual
authority in religious matters; 2. The primary importance
of free scientific investigation; 3. The rejection of the
belief in Israel's restoration. These resolutions will be
hailed by all spiritually-minded Christians of every sect
and denomination, including all who love God and maintain the authority of His revealed mind and will in the
Holy Scriptures, as the one and only rule of moral culture
and civilization; as pointing in a most decided manner to
the first ray of enlightenment demonstrated by these three
brilliant resolutions, that have burst through the dark and
impenetrable clouds of prejudice and educational bias that
has beclouded the understandings, dulled and obscured the
intellectual faculties of that highly interesting nation, the
children of Israel, who, to this day, are a standing monument and most convincing proof of the unquestionable
veracity of the Holy Scriptures, the one living Lord God
Jehovah of Israel, His judgments, righteousness, covenant
love and mercy, for "Salvation is of the Jews." The
most happy results that will accrue, with the blessing of
Jehovah, for the advancement of Israel's welfare will be
acknowledged with gratitude by all who are interested in
the fulfilment of Scripture, by the universal recognition of
these resolutions, after a period extending over eighteen
centuries of persecution, cruelty, subjection, and banish-
ment; not so much from the consideration of proselytizing
the Jews to the faith of the New Covenant (Jer. xxxi. 31—34;

see also Isaac Leeser's and Dr. Benisch's translations),
which they cannot possibly receive but by the special and
peculiar gift of Jehovah Himself (Prov. xx. 12 ; Isaiah
vi. 9, 10, 11), but from the encouragement and stimulus it
will impart to those inquiring minds who have hitherto
been bound and shackled by a blind and dogmatic interpretation of the plain literal statements of the Scriptures,
while contra-indicated both by the context and the unmis-
takeable corroborative evidence of the events and circumstances recorded by the pages of history, as reliable as the
literal testimony of the Bible itself, from the confirmation
imparted thereby to its truth. But as I shall have occasion to
notice this more fully, by producing evidence from Jewish
writers to expose the caprices and impositions of priestcraft
to which this interesting people have been subjected by
their own teachers, without any allusion to the New Testament, beyond reference to those passages that immediately
and literally support the literal testimony of the Old Testament, I will content myself by taking this opportunity
to accept the challenge of the Chief Rabbi of the
Bayswater Synagogue, put forth in a course of Sermons,
published by Trübner and Co. In Sermon IV., p. 54, this
writer says : "Now, I boldly challenge every professor of
the Christian faith to tell me where it is stated that the
prophet like unto Moses was to declare a new revelation."
I will here state, as a preliminary observation, that my
motive in writing is not to address my remarks to any
individual personally, but strictly to principles for the vindication of the truth of Scripture, without going over
ground occupied by men of superior abilities, education,
spiritual knowledge, and discernment, to which I neither
make nor claim the slightest pretensions; therefore, in
endeavouring to reply to this challenge, I shall meet
it generally as the avowed fundamental principle of
Judaism; and in replying to it I will undertake to prove,
from the plain literal testimony of the Law and the Prophets, that by obliterating the literal evidence from the
Scriptures, pointing to the Most Holy Trinity of three
distinct, co-eternal, co-equal persons in one undivided
Jehovah, it would thereby reduce the Scriptures to a mass
of confused contradiction and heathen mythology ; therefore, without the slightest attempt to solve or explain this
most unutterable and incomprehensible mystery as to the

manner and possibility of three distinct eternal persons existing in one undivided unity from all eternity, beyond proving that it is a revealed truth that can only be received by God's own special and peculiar gift of faith as declared by Moses, " The secret things belong unto the Lord our God : but those things which are revealed belong unto us and to our children for ever, that we may do all the words of this law " (Deut. xxix. 29 ; also Dr. Benisch's translation, under the supervision of the Chief Rabbi, verse 28, in the Hebrew Bible, and in the Jewish translation of Isaac Leeser).

Since controversy but too often leads to the development of a spirit more calculated to obscure and overthrow the object its end and design is intended to vindicate and establish, I will here state that it is not my object to impute wrong motives to our Jewish brethren, nor yet to strive for the mastery, for I have personal acquaintances who are Jews whom I regard and respect as friends ; and I believe the Jews generally are not aware of the interest and sympathy borne towards them by every right-minded Christian ; for who can behold that handsome and beautifully-featured people, possessing the highest order of intellect and mental qualification that characterizes their physical and social aspect as a nation, but with feelings of sorrow and pity to behold their scattered condition, bearing the strongest evidences of a powerful constitutional organization in themselves, yet without any form of government or country they can call their own. Nor can the idea of Polytheism be more revolting and unscriptural to the understanding of the strictest Pharisee, Rabbi, or ruler of a synagogue than it is to the spiritual comprehension of a Christian, as may be seen from the words of the Nazarene Himself: " The first of all the commandments is, Hear, O Israel ; the Lord our God is one Lord : and thou shalt love the Lord thy God with all thy heart, and with all thy soul, and with all thy mind, and with all thy strength : this is the first commandment. And the second is like, namely this, Thou shalt love thy neighbour as thyself. There is none other commandment greater than these " (Mark xii. 29, 30, 31).

The doctrine of the vicarious atonement is disputed by the Jews as violently as that of the Most Holy Trinity ; therefore, in order to reply to the above challenge, it will be necessary to prove that Moses wrote of nothing else but of the Trinity of persons in the undivided unity of one Jehovah, יהוה, pronounced אדני, Ardownoy. If no other literal evidence existed to testify of the vicarious atonement of Jehovah the Eternal Son of God, besides that contributed by the consonants and vowels of the Hebrew alphabet, that alone would be sufficient to enable any inquiring, intelligent mind to discern that a special object, far more exalted and sublime, was clearly pointed to by the characters through which the Most Holy Law of God has been handed down and preserved to us, together with the testimony of the Prophets, than that of merely contributing a medium of perpetuating and conveying our ideas from generation to generation.

SECTION II.

ALEPH, א, AND TAU, ת, OR ALPHA, A, AND OMEGA Ω, THE FIRST AND THE LAST.

IF we turn to Psalm cxix., we find twenty-two divisions, each division preceded by the name of one of the twenty-two consonant letters of the Hebrew alphabet, in their proper alphabetical order, as spelt and pronounced in English. Each of these letters possesses its own signification, not merely in an hieroglyphical sense, but in many instances actually representing the outline of the object of which it contributes the name, as may be ascertained by referring to the Hebrew grammars of Jewish authority, and that of Gesenius, which is admitted to be the most classical by the author of the course of sermons preached in the Bayswater Synagogue (vide Sermon II). I will not here occupy time and space by giving the letters in detail, with their various significations, which would not be evidence sufficiently conclusive to those who might be disposed to heap together the conflicting disputes of commentators and pre-judiced writers, whose opinions and differences cannot go beyond convincing their own adherents and supporters. I shall, therefore, confine myself to the grammar of the most Holy Scriptures as the lexicon for the solution of any apparent difficulty in the signification of words, by the production of those passages in which the same words occur, to determine and establish their etymology. Therefore I shall notice the testimony of each letter that may have any reference to the subject in its proper place, as occasion may require.

Now, it is quite clear to the perception of all who can read that there is not a particle of evidence upon record to show, or in any way justify, an inference that the art of writing was known to be in existence before sin entered into the world by the disobedience of our forefather Adam. Taking this for granted, without combating with the objections of Cabalistic theories, I address my observations to men who may be regarded as sound orthodox adherents of Judaism, who reject every theory but what they conceive to be based upon sound Scriptural principles. Whatever speculative theories may be advanced concerning the book or prophecy of Enoch, it is not my province to combat with here. I believe it is generally admitted by Jews, as well as Christians, that the characteristic form of the letters of the Hebrew language now in our possession are faithful representations of the first and most ancient of all alphabets, first portrayed by the finger of Jehovah Himself upon Mount Sinai, when He wrote the Decalogue with His own most holy fingers upon the two tables of stone, and delivered them to Moses (Exodus xxxi. 18). It is essentially necessary to notice these particulars very carefully and attentively, as we proceed with this inquiry, because it is clearly stated that God wrote the two tables of the testimony with His own finger, and gave them to Moses. I here give the passage from the Jewish translation of Isaac Leeser: "And He gave unto Moses, when He had finished speaking with him upon Mount Sinai, the two tables of the testimony, tables of stone, inscribed with the finger of God" (Exodus xxxi. 18). Here, then, it is clear that God did actually write, and that it is recorded that He had a finger as the medium with which he wrote, and that this word "finger," אצבע, in this passage, is the same word by which the finger of a man is expressed, as in Lev. iv. 6, &c.; and upon such testimony as this I shall prove that Jehovah did actually have a distinct form and similitude, in which He appeared as a distinct and visible person to those with whom He established His covenant, both before and after He dictated the Hebrew alphabet to Moses, and wrote the form

of its characters with His own finger, by which we shall see
the perfect harmony and agreement of that passage where
it is recorded that God declared to Moses that no man
should see His face and live, without seeking to support
Cabalistic theories, but from the clear testimony of the
Scriptures.

The first letter of the Hebrew alphabet, א, *Aleph*, signifies an ox (*vide* the grammars of Hurwitz and Gesenius);
but how shall we prove that this signification is not an
invention of men, and dependent upon tradition for its
only support? If we refer to Isaiah xxx. 24, we find the
word "Aleph" (an ox) used in its plural form, אלפים, is
rendered oxen in the Authorized Version, and also in the
Jewish translation of Leeser. By this it is unmistakeably
clear that the very first letter of the Hebrew alphabet,
which is the first letter that occurs in the Ten Commandments,
written by the finger of God upon Sinai, and also the first
letter that occurs in the name of God, אלהים, Ehlohim,
points to a *subject of sacrifice*, an ox, the chief subject of
Jewish ceremonial sacrifice, and an emblem of obedience.

The last letter, ת, Tau (or Tov), is defined to signify a
cross by the Hebrew grammarian Gesenius, an authority
claimed by the author of the course of Sermons preached
in the Bayswater Synagogue, in support of his assertions.
Hurwitz and Hebrew grammarians generally define Tov as *a
boundary*, the *end*, a *mark*, a *sign;* but we are not dependent
upon the definitions of lexicographers or grammarians,
because the Phœnicians, Greeks, and Romans took the form
of the letter T, from the signification of the Hebrew consonant Tov, to which it is the equivalent corresponding
letter in sound and power. Great differences of opinion
exist concerning the original form of the Roman cross : some
consider its form to have resembled the letter T, with the
horizontal beam supported upon the summit of the per-
pendicular piece of timber, without any projecting portion
above ; but the circumstances connected are strongly in
favour of the usual form, because of the superscription
Pontius Pilate fixed upon (the projecting piece above) the
cross. But the most conclusive evidence is contributed by
the form of the letter Tov upon the coins of the Maccabees.
After the Babylonish captivity of the Jews, upon such
coins it may be seen represented by the form of a cross.
In Arabic it also signifies a mark in the form of a cross,

put upon the necks of camels (*vide* Bagster's Hebrew and Chaldee Lexicon). This letter, as spelt, תו or תוה, constitutes a word of itself, used as a verb and a noun; in Dan. iii. 24, it is written in Chaldee, signifying to be *amazed, astonished :* in Hebrew it signifies a mark or sign, to make marks, to scrabble, as in 1 Sam. xxi. 14; Ezek. ix. 4, in Psalm lxxviii. 41 : it signifies to limit; metaphorically it is used to signify to provoke, to wound, &c. The connexion of which is obvious ; for instance, a person who is crossed, mentally or physically, is grieved or provoked in consequence (*vide* the translations of Leeser and Dr. Benisch). Thus, while the first letter of the alphabet points to a subject of sacrifice, the last letter points to the manner in which that sacrifice was appointed to be offered as the boundary or end of the types and shadows of the ceremonial law, which have ceased to exist ever since, because Jerusalem, together with the temple, was totally destroyed by Titus thirty-seven years after the Nazarene was cut off, according to the predictions of the Spirit of God through the prophets.

The letters Aleph and Tau, את, form the sign of the accusative case, and the most frequently used of the Hebrew particles. Before I proceed to prove from the Scriptures that God has a distinct form and image, similitude, and likeness, by whom He appeared to the patriarchs of old, and its perfect harmony with Deut. iv. 12, 15, it will be necessary to prove the plurality of אלהים, Ehlohim, when used to discriminate the person of EL-SHADDAI, or God Almighty ; and that if the plural noun Ehlohim, when applied to Jehovah, does not point to the three distinct eternal persons of the undivided unity of Jehovah, the literal testimony of the Scriptures could not be depended upon, since the literal testimony of the Scriptures is a point so earnestly contended for by the Jews, particularly in those passages referring to the Messiah.

In the refutation of this objection, it will be seen that the doctrines of Christianity vindicate the Scriptures and the revelation of the undivided unity of Jehovah more signally than the doctrines of Judaism; inasmuch as the sole object of Christianity is to exalt the God of Abraham, Isaac, and Jacob as the only one true God, who is Aleph and Tov, or, according to the Greek version of the Scriptures called the Septuagint, Alpha and Omega—"the first and the last,"

(Isaiah xliv. 6), who says, "I, even I, am יהוה, Jehovah; and beside me there is no Saviour" (Isaiah xliii. 11); "I am אל, God, and there is none else; I am אלהים, Ehlohim, and there is none like me, declaring the end from the beginning, and from ancient times the things that are not yet done, saying, My council shall stand, and I will do all my pleasure" (Isaiah xlvi. 9, 10).

SECTION III.

EHLOHIM.

THE plural noun Ehlohim, when employed in the Scriptures to discriminate the divine person of Jehovah as the one true God or Ehlohim, it occasionally governs plural verbs construed with plural adjectives, as in Hos. xii. 4, 5; Isaiah vi. 8; Gen. i. 26, iii. 22, xi. 7, xx. 13, xxxv. 7; Psalm lviii. 12, &c. The vocabulary of the Hebrew language does not possess another word to express Gods (in the plural number) besides EHLOHIM; for proof of this, in the Hebrew Bible the plural noun Ehlohim is employed to express idols and false gods in one hundred and ninety-five passages, which may be ascertained by referring to the Authorized English Version and the Jewish translations of Leeser and Dr. Benisch; the following passages will afford sufficient proof: Gen. xxxi. 30—32, xxv. 2—4; Exod. xii. 12, xviii. 11, xx. 3; Jer. v. 7, xvi. 20. The same noun is employed to distinguish judges in the plural number in Exod. xxii. 8, 9, and verse 28 (*vide* margin) of the Authorized Version.

Thus from the Chief Rabbi's own authorities the noun אלהים, Ehlohim, is clearly defined to be distinctly the plural form of אל, El, or אלה, Ehloh, and the reason why it is not uniformly and continuously construed with plural verbs, adverbs, and adjectives is clearly communicated by the Shemang, and throughout the Law and the Prophets by the distinct Eternal Person of the divine Word, declaring that He is one with Ehlohim, that He is Ehlohim, and besides Him there is none else; therefore this mysterious oneness with Ehlohim would evidently be lost to the comprehension of man if continuously construed with plural verbs, adverbs, and adjectives. In Gen. i. 26, it is written, "And Ehlohim said, Let us make man in our own image, after our likeness." The construction here is admitted by the Chief Rabbi to be plural. Two passages from the Law will sufficiently establish the plurality of Ehlohim as a point beyond the reach of all dispute by those who admit the divine authenticity and inspiration of the Scriptures. "Thou shalt have no אלהים אחרים [other Ehlohim] before me." "Thou shalt not bow thyself down to THEM nor serve THEM; for I Jehovah, thy Ehlohim, am a jealous (אל, EL) God" (Exod. xx. 3—5). In this commandment the plural noun Ehlohim, construed with plural verbs, adverbs, and pronouns, is used to discriminate false gods or lifeless idols; while the singular form אל, EL, is used to distinguish Jehovah as the one, true, living Ehlohim; this affords conclusive proof of the plurality of Ehlohim.

The next point is to prove that the plural noun Ehlohim, when applied to Jehovah, is not merely a term limited to an expression of plural excellence, but actually expressing a plurality of eternal persons in the unity of one undivided Jehovah. In Gen. iii. 22, the language of Jehovah Ehlohim is this: "Behold the man is become כאחד ממנו, AS ONE OF US." The construction of this sentence admits of no possible inference that it is merely an expression of plural excellence, but most positively forbids any such conclusion, because in that case Jehovah Ehlohim would have declared man to have become equal in plural excellence with Jehovah Himself, and would thus have acknowledged fallen rebellious man to have become equal with Himself, which is a self-evident contradiction to Eccles. vii. 20; Psalm li. 5, to say nothing whatever of the literal expression and idiom of the Hebrew text, clearly pointing to the discrimination of ONE person from a plural number. Had the Hebrew have been כמונו, or כמנו, as we, or like ourselves, as in Gen. xxxiv. 15, then but little could be proved from the literal testimony of this passage to overthrow an inference of an expression of plural excellence beyond the contradiction it would have conveyed, because we know that man has not become equal in power and majesty and plural excellence with God. Man, by his robbery from the tree of knowledge, had only achieved a limited knowledge—i.e., that of knowing good and evil—while man had no right, upon righteous ground,

to know anything beyond the most implicit obedience to
his Creator; hence fallen man, by his sin, became like
God only so far as to discern between good and evil. But
man is without the power of God to resist evil, which none
but the almighty power of Jehovah and His Spirit can
withstand; and the fact of man not being in possession of
an unaided independent power to resist evil in and of himself (Psalm cxxxix.; Jer. x. 23, xvii. 9) is another proof
that he has not become equal in plural excellence with
Ehlohim, because man is dependent upon the Word and
Spirit of God to keep him, and graciously constrain him to
obedience (Psalm xxxvii. 23, 24). According to the Chief
Rabbi's own admission, man was created in the image of
Ehlohim, proving that Ehlohim has a visible form and
similitude, of which man's person and form is the likeness
(Gen. i. 26, 27). Thus man, independent of his robbing
God of the knowledge of good and evil, physically resem-
bles the external form of the One Person of the Godhead of
Ehlohim, according to the words of the serpent: "Ye
shall be כאלהים, as Ehlohim, knowing good and evil"
(Gen. iii. 5); and, as admitted by Jehovah Ehlohim,
" Behold the man is become as one of us, to know good
and evil" (ver. 22); from the consideration of which the
Psalmist writes by the diction of Spirit Ehlohim, " I have
said, YE ARE EHLOHIM, or gods; and all of you are children
of the Most High. But ye shall die like men, and fall
like one of the princes " (Psalm lxxxii. 6, 7). Therefore
the word אחד (Akhod), 'one,' in the language of Jehovah
Ehlohim, when He said, "Behold the man is become as
one of us," clearly points to one particular person as a distinct person, discriminated from the other two in the Trinity
of the Godhead.

SECTION IV.

THE SHEMANG.

"Hear, O Israel: Jehovah our Ehlohim is ONE Jehovah."—DEUT. vi. 4.

IN Leeser's Bible it is rendered thus, "Hear, O Israel! The LORD our God is the ONE Eternal Being." Dr. Benisch in his translation renders it, "Hear, O Israel: The Eternal our God the Eternal is One." The Chief Rabbi of the Bayswater Synagogue defines the word אחד, One, in this passage to imply *One, without any division of parts* (*vide* Sermon I., p. 9). This definition, in its application to Jehovah Ehlohim, *cannot righteously be disputed*, the revelation of which it is the one sole object of the Scriptures to convey. The exhortation to hear and believe that Jehovah Ehlohim is One was uttered that the Israelites should have no ground for the slightest inference of Polytheism from the unquestionable plurality of Ehlohim and its construction with plural verbs, adverbs, and adjectives, a point which Moses was directed to so carefully clear up, after recording the language of the Trinity at the creation of man, when Ehlohim said, "Let us make man in our image, after our likeness." He wrote in the next verse the unity of the three persons in the Godhead by the employment of the usual construction in the singular number, to counteract any inference of the three persons constituting more than one and the same God: "So Ehlohim created man in His own image, in the image of Ehlohim created He him; male and female created He them" (Gen. i. 26, 27). To confirm this, the Shemang was uttered, Hear, O Israel, Jehovah, our plural Ehlohim, is a united Jehovah, or one Jehovah, because after sin entered the world man can know nothing of God but through the medium of Messenger Ehlohim (rendered the Angel of God), or Messenger Jehovah (rendered the Angel of the Lord), in whose image the plurality of divine persons dwell as One Ehlohim Jehovah, because out of or away from Messenger or Mediator Jehovah no man can see God's face and live (Exod. xxxiii. 20). Yet it is distinctly recorded that Hagar (Gen. xvi. 13), Jacob

(Gen xxxii. 28—30), and Moses (Exod. xxxiii. 11; Numb. xiv. 14; Deut. v. 4, xxxiv. 10) all saw God face to face, and were not consumed, because they saw and beheld God in the divine person of מלאך פניו, *the Angel of His presence* (Isaiah lxiii. 9), which is literally the messenger of HIS FACE, which I shall prove from the Chief Rabbi's own definite and correct rendering of the words יהוה הוא, i.e., *the Lord Himself*, in Isaiah vii. 14. Here the Chief Rabbi admits that the personal pronoun הוא, construed with the sacred Tetragrammaton, Jehovah, is to be rendered, " *The Lord Himself*" (*vide* Sermon II., pages 16—19; also the Jewish translation of Leeser, Isaiah vii. 14). This is substantiated and vindicated in the account of the appearance of Messenger Jehovah as (איש) a man to Manoah and his wife (Judges xiii.), " And Messenger Jehovah said unto Manoah, Though thou detain me, I will not eat of thy bread: and if thou wilt offer a burnt offering, thou must offer it unto Jehovah. כי לא־ידע מנוח כי־מלאך יהוה הוא, " For Manoah knew not that the ANGEL WAS JEHOVAH," or, according to the Chief Rabbi's definition of יהוה הוא, it may be read as follows: For Manoah knew not that the *Angel was the Lord Himself*, defined by the prophet Isaiah to be the Angel of Jehovah's face or presence, who constituted the One Jehovah. And when Manoah asked, What is thy name, Messenger Jehovah said, Why askest thou after my name? והוא פלאי,* AND HE MY WONDERFUL, (see margin); "so Manoah took a kid with a meat offering and offered it upon a rock unto the Lord (who) did wondrously; and Manoah and his wife looked on. For it came to pass when the flame went up toward heaven from off the altar, that Messenger Jehovah ascended in the flame of the altar." "Then Manoah knew that the Angel יהוה הוא, *was Jehovah*, or, according to the Chief Rabbi's definition, it may be read, Then Manoah knew that the Angel was *Jehovah Himself*. " And Manoah said unto his wife, We shall surely die, because אלהים ראינו, WE HAVE SEEN

---

* Hebrew grammarians tell us that there is no neuter gender in the Hebrew grammar. Whatever construction may be put upon the points, this noun פלא, *wonderful*, cannot be read correctly as an adjective, because it is clearly a substantive from its construction with the personal pronoun HE, and the *conjunctive* ו, Vav; see also Isaiah ix. 6, and Gen. xviii. 14, where the demonstrative definite article is smothered up by a reputed form of conjugation Niphal.

EHLOHIM." Here our Jewish brethren must admit that the united testimony of Manoah and his wife claims our reliance in preference to any further explanations of men, because we are neither to take from nor to add to the Word of God (Deut. iv. 2, xii. 32); especially as the law declares a thing to be established by the testimony of two or three witnesses (Deut. xix. 15).

This explanation of Manoah confirms the Shemang that the plurality of Ehlohim constitutes one Jehovah, and at once disposes of the difficulty of the import of the passage in Isaiah xxvi. 4, noticed by the Jewish grammarian Solomon Lyon, teacher of Hebrew to the Universities of Oxford and Cambridge, and Eton College, who, in his grammar, interprets this verse as follows : "For with יְהּ, Yoh (JAH), the Lord created the world," remarking that "the meaning of this verse appears very unintelligible." The same author remarks upon Psalm xxxiii. 6, by admitting the divine personality of the person of the mediatorial Word as follows : "'By the word of the Lord were the heavens made, and by the breath of His mouth all the host of them.' The difficulty of this verse is, first, to know the word by which the heavens were made ; secondly, how to apply the latter part of this verse to the Deity." But, as further proofs from Jewish authorities as to the distinct personality of the Word will be given in another section, these are sufficient to prove that the Shemang is an exhortation to believe by faith a certain truth that cannot be received and believed by the carnal mind of man, because for a man to understand or comprehend the great name Jehovah Ehlohim by the discernment of his own judgment between good and evil that he robbed from Jehovah Ehlohim, it is altogether out of the question, since God declared by Jeremiah that the heart of man is deceitful above all things, and desperately wicked to such an extent that none but the Lord can know it (Jer. xvii. 9, 10); and that there are none that do good and sin not (Eccles. vii. 20). This will account for the earnest appeal of שְׁמַע, Hear, believe, i.e., understand for a certain and positive truth that Jehovah, our plural Ehlohim of more than one distinct person, is essentially one in undivided eternal unity, without any division of parts ; otherwise, what necessity would there be for this earnest appeal to believe what no reasonable man could disbelieve if he were to try ? for who can deny with

B

the answer of a good conscience that one is one ?· Therefore it can require no effort to believe what would be incompatible with the dictates of the divine gift of reason to
disbelieve. It is in opposition to the sin-contaminated
knowledge and discernment of man that the Shemang was
uttered, that the incomprehensible mystery of the oneness
of the Godhead of Jehovah may be received and believed.
In Ezek xi. 19, it is written, וְנָתַתִּי לָהֶם לֵב אֶחָד, "And I
will give THEM ONE heart." This is a promise made by
the Lord God to the remnant of the house of Israel, whom
He sanctified to save under the new covenant (Jer. xxxi.
31—33). Here God has promised to give His people,
collectively, gathered from all the tribes and nations of the
earth, but אֶחָד, *one* heart, *i.e.*, one single individual heart,
as defined by the Chief Rabbi to signify *without any
division of parts*, by which one. heart whole nations and
tribes collectively shall be actuated. Incompatible as this
is with the dictates of carnal reason, it is admitted, and
produced by the Jews as evidence to overthrow the plurality
of Ehlohim. The Hebrew word אֶחָד, employed to express
and record the unity of Jehovah, is precisely the same word
that is used in Gen. ii. 24: "Therefore shall a man leave
his father and his mother, and cleave unto his wife ; and
they shall be לְבָשָׂר אֶחָד, ONE FLESH," or, according to
Leeser's Bible, "they become one flesh." Thus, according
to the Jewish definition of this word אֶחָד, one, here are two
distinct persons declared to be one by an undivided union,
without any division of parts; therefore, though this definition admits of no refutation in its application to express
the undivided unity of Jehovah Ehlohim, yet when this
word אֶחָד is employed under other circumstances, the
definition of the Chief Rabbi is incorrect, from the fact of
its having a plural form, אֲחָדִים, rendered *few* in Gen.
xxvii. 44, &c. Dr. Benisch renders it in the same manner :
therefore, if the Chief Rabbi's definition be accepted as the
only and exclusive signification, we must read *ones* for the
plural form of this word, אֶחָד; thus 'days *ones*' and
'*words ones*,' instead of its primitive signification ; thus united
days, united speech, Gen. xi. 1 : but if, on the other hand,
אֶחָד, Akhod, be rendered according to its primary signification, "united," its meaning will be vindicated by its own
expression of the sense of the sentence or passage ; for instance, God called the light and the darkness, יוֹם אֶחָד, one

day. Here the Chief Rabbi's definition, *without any division
of parts*, fails to support itself, because God declared that
two distinct and separate elements, light and darkness,
between which God Himself put a division to distinguish
one element from the other, self-evidently constituting a
division of parts, to be discriminated by אֶחָד, which, if read
according to its primitive signification, the meaning is
vindicated and the sense retained; thus the light and the
darkness were a *united* day, or one day, usually rendered
the "first day" (Gen. i. 5); but by no means without any
division of parts, because God declared in this instance
that two elements constituted one unity. This proves the
Chief Rabbi's definition to be only a derivative signification when used under other circumstances. And, again, in
the following texts, if *united* is read for "one," the sense
is fully preserved and the meaning vindicated: Ezek. xi.
19, "I will give them a *united* heart;" Gen. ii. 24, "And
they shall be *united* flesh;" Deut. vi. 4, "Jehovah our
[plural] Elhohim is Jehovah *united*," or a united Jehovah.
Dr. Benisch and Isaac Leeser both render this word by
"*united*" in Gen. xlix. 6; therefore if this word אֶחָד is
indiscriminately rendered by its *derivative* signification,
one, asserting that the word contra-indicates any inference of a division of parts, such an interpretation
cannot be supported by the syntax of the Scriptures
as the sole and exclusive signification, which must be
supported by the circumstances of the context or the
general teaching of the Scripture. This word is by no
means an exception. For instance, the root נָחַם, in Gen.
vi. 6, 7, and Jer. viii. 6, signifies to repent by feeling
the pain of remorse; while in Gen. v. 29, the same
root is employed to express comfort as a derivative signification, being the very opposite meaning to that indicated
by its primary form. Wherever we find an appeal recorded in the Word of God, exhorting those to whom it is
addressed to believe and receive the truth it asserts, we
may be sure that something is conveyed for the spiritual
discernment of those to whom it is directed that cannot be
comprehended by the reasoning faculties of the sin-contaminated carnal mind of man; for proof of which no
passage of the Holy Scriptures affords a more remarkable
instance than the passage termed by the Jews the *Shemang*
(*i. e., Hear*), "Hear, O Israel, the LORD our God is one

B 2

Lord" (Deut. vi. 4); which they produce with such parallel
passages as the following: "My glory will I not give to
another" (Isaiah xlii. 8); "I will not give my glory unto
another" (xlviii. 11); "For I am God, and there is none
else; I am God, and there is none like me" (xlvi. 9); "I,
even I, am the Lord; and beside me there is no saviour"
(xliii. 11); "And there is no God else beside me; a just
God and a saviour; there is none beside me. Look unto
me, and be ye saved, all the ends of the earth; for I am
God, and there is none else. I have sworn by myself; the
word is gone out of my mouth in righteousness, and shall
not return, That unto me every knee shall bow, every
tongue shall swear," &c. (xlv. 21—23), considering these
passages as the most conclusive evidence to justify their
rejection of all belief in the advent and divinity of the
Messiah as a distinct person in the undivided Trinity of
Ehlohim Jehovah, while they are unconscious of the tre-
mendous fact that all these declarations are uttered through
the medium of the distinct person of the Eternal Son of
God, the divine Word, whose government continues to
spread over the earth as the waters cover the sea, and to
whom every knee, without exception, is made to bow,
because His children are all made willing in the day of
His power (Psalm cx. 3). The same person, called in
other places Messenger Jehovah and Messenger Ehlohim,
usually translated the Angel of the Lord and the Angel of
God, who appeared to Abraham, Isaac, Jacob, and Moses,
and claimed the title of God, and through whom the Lord
God communicated with them, and in whom they saw God
face to face, as I shall prove in its place, and its perfect
harmony with the words of God to Moses, "No man shall
see my face and live." Consider the language uttered by
the divine person of the Word, who communicates or
speaks through the prophet, how this medium of communication declares that He is Ehlohim; the intense persuasion of the language, the pleading, the appealing, the
yearning on the behalf of those to whom it is addressed,
"I will not give my glory unto another;" "for I am God,
and there is none else." But if we refer to the second
book of Moses, we find it recorded that this one living God
of Israel did actually give His glory to another, which in
no way contradicts these statements recorded in the Book
of Isaiah, but at once vindicates and confirms their veracity.

God declared to Moses that He would send מַלְאָךְ, messenger, before the children of Israel to keep them in the way, at the same time יְהוָה, Jehovah, or the Eternal, declared that His name was in this מַלְאָךְ, angel or messenger. Now the name of Jehovah expresses His glory and eternity as fully as can be expressed through the medium of alphabetical characters. So glorious and sacred is this most holy name that an adherent of Judaism is not permitted to utter it, as before observed; indeed, so incomprehensibly holy is this name יְהוָה, that Jehovah Himself could not find a name more glorious to swear by. " Behold I have sworn by my great name, saith the Lord" (Jer. xliv. 26). Therefore His name constitutes the honour and glory of Jehovah, who declared that He would not give His glory to another; while it is recorded in the Pentateuch that He actually did give His glory to another. He gave it to the angel of His presence. And we find this angel or messenger of His name and presence so jealous of the glory of this name that he (THE ANGEL) would not pardon transgressions under a covenant of works, requiring that implicit obedience demanded by the most holy law of God the honour of which this angel was so jealous. "Behold I send Messenger before thee, to keep thee on the way, and to bring thee unto the place which I have prepared. Beware of him and obey his voice, disobey him not; for he will not pardon your transgression : because MY NAME IS IN HIM. But if thou wilt carefully hearken to his voice, and do all that I speak ; then will I be an enemy unto thy enemies, and afflict those that afflict thee" (Exod. xxiii. 20—22; *vide* Isaac Leeser's Jewish translation). Here the angel is declared by Jehovah Himself to be the medium of communication, in whom God had placed His glorious name, יְהוָה, and that Israel was to obey this angel as the voice of Jehovah, who had previously declared that Israel should have no other Ehlohim [gods] before him (Exod. xx. 3). Here let it be observed that the indisputable fact of the name of יְהוָה, Jehovah, being in the מַלְאָךְ, angel or messenger, is so clearly expressed in the Hebrew by the selection of particular words from its vocabulary that clearly define the name of Jehovah, or the Eternal, to constitute an undivided unseparable attribute of the angel, כִּי שְׁמִי בְּקִרְבּוֹ, *i.e.*, " because my name is in him." "In all their affliction He was afflicted, and the angel of His presence saved them" (Isaiah lxiii. 9). Therefore it is very clear that if the undivided unity of כלאך, the messenger here alluded to, is rejected from being a distinct person in the Trinity of אלהים, Ehlohim, these passages would clearly contradict each other, and be perfectly unintelligible.

SECTION V.

ABRAHAM'S FAITH IN THE SHEMANG.

If the eighteenth chapter of Genesis bo carefully read, it will be seen to express that the Eternal appeared to Abraham as three men, who personified the Triune Jehovah; and let it be particularly noticed that in the twenty-second verse it does not state that the *three* men turned their faces from thence, but "*the men*," and if we follow them to the next chapter, we find it recorded that only TWO angels entered Sodom: now, where was the third? This twenty-second verse clearly informs us, as it stands, according to the original Hebrew text,

ויפנו משם האנשים וילכו סדמה ויהוה עודני עמד לפני אברהם

"And the men turned their faces from thence, and went towards Sodom : *and Jehovah, YET I, stood before Abraham.*" This is the language of the eternal Son of God, as written by Moses at the dictation of the distinct person of Jehovah the *Word*, which was altered by the decrees of the Scribes = Tikun Sopherim, to the present reading, which is still retained in the Hebrew, to obviate what was regarded as an offensive anthropomorphism, as noted by the Massorah ; therefore the original reading that when the men departed* "*Jehovah stood still before Abraham,*" substantiates the import of the whole chapter, that Jehovah was personified by three men ; for when the two departed, "Jehovah stood still before Abraham," and only two angels entered Sodom, וילך יהוה כאשר כלה לדבר אל־אברהם, which is literally, "And the Eternal went as soon as He had finished with the Word unto Abraham." Now, this communication between Abraham and the Eternal was through the distinct person of Jehovah the Eternal Son, because Abraham addresses

* *Vide* Jacob Ben Chajim's Introduction to the Rabbinic Bible, by Dr. Ginsburg.

the three in the singular number. (What have the Jews to
say about terms of plural excellence here?) It proves
Abraham's faith in the Shemang that the three persons of
Ehlohim are one and the same Jehovah, because throughout the interview and conversation Jehovah addresses
Abraham; so that it is difficult for our carnal reason to
understand beyond what we can receive by faith, as
Abraham did; carefully avoiding all speculations of our
opinions as to the probability or possibility of anything
connected with divine revelation. Rashi admits that
Abraham addressed these three men as one, and that they
communicated with Abraham as one and the same. The
fourteenth verse clearly reveals this in a still more remarkable manner. In order to prove the import of its literal expression, I am necessitated to give the passage in the original,

היפלא מיהוה דבר למועד אשוב אליך כעת חיה ולשרה בן.

In this passage the expression היפלא, translated SHALL
IT BE DIFFICULT, is formed from the Hebrew root פלא,
used in Isaiah ix. 6, that signifies *wonderful*, "inter-
cessor," "mediator," and "separator," and is the same
word which the angel who appeared to Manoah declared
to constitute His name Wonderful—in the margin. Let
the reader carefully compare and consider this, because
with a little attention it can be comprehended. Now we
know a wonderful thing must be a hard or difficult thing,
in order to constitute a wonderful thing; therefore, while
we see its sense is truthfully expressed to a spiritual mind,
yet its *full meaning* cannot be literally expressed by rendering it "Shall anything be too hard," though that is
one sense clearly conveyed by the context; yet it is more
literal to render the verse thus, "*This wonderful Word from
Jehovah (at or) for the appointed time, I will return unto thee
according to the time of life, and Sarah shall have a son.*" Here
the distinct personality of the Word is clearly defined by
the substantive דבר (Word), which is expressed in such
a manner by the particle מן used as a prefix to Jehovah,
that indicates the divine person of the Eternal Word to
centre in Jehovah as the distinct part and source of the
same substance. Gesenius defines מן to be a preposition
of motion. [Properly part of a thing, as a *partitive* preposition, designating a part taken from a whole; hence the
idea of departing, removing from, away from, anything or
place.] *Vide* Grammar, section 151. This particle also

expresses comparison, but as no negative whatever occurs in Genesis xviii. 14, it cannot there be rendered as the comparative, if the literal expression of the text be adhered to, otherwise it would fail to support the idiom of Jer. xxxii. 17, 27. The letter ה prefixed to the noun פלא, Wonderful, is so generally admitted by Hebrew grammarians to constitute the sign of the definite article or demonstrative letter, that it is needless to produce Scripture proof; and even admitting the verbal signification of the word Wonderful, verbs prefixed by י, Yod, are frequently used as proper names; for instance, צחק, to laugh, prefixed by Yod, forms Isaac, which if prefixed by the definite article or sign of demonstration, it would have to be read the Isaac, or this Isaac; so in Genesis xviii. 14, "this Wonderful." But if it is insisted upon by scholars that this expression יפלא is the third person singular, masculine gender, future tense of the verb occurring in conjugation Niphal, as a student I am willing to give place to the superior judgment of scholars, so far as the grammatical structure of the verse is concerned, for even in that case it supports the reading I have here given, because under these circumstances it would have to be rendered as a passive verb in the future tense, He shall be Wonderful. Whether the prefix ה be rendered as a sign of interrogation or demonstration, it is not my purpose to contend for, because the point Khatuph-parsah may be found in many instances to be rendered as indicating demonstration. It is quite certain the root Wonderful as used in Isaiah ix. 6, as a noun, is also used in Genesis xviii. 14, where it is followed by the name of the ETERNAL, as the equal source, or part and parcel of this Wonderful; then follows the noun דבר, WORD, by which the person of "this Wonderful" is revealed throughout the Scriptures as the divine person of the Word of the Lord: see 1 Kings xviii. 31, where the Eternal personality of the Word is defined to be the divine being who wrestled with Jacob: compare this with Genesis xxxii. 28, 30, and Hosea xii. 4, 5. Therefore it is clear that in Genesis xviii. 14, the language of the Trinity is recorded as uttered by the divine speaker or Word as the medium of communication to Abraham.

The same Biblical method of definition that defines the expression היפלא, The HE shall be Wonderful, or This Wonderful, also defines the Tetragrammaton Jehovah, יהוה, from

the Biblical fact that the root, הוה, of this name being a
verb and also a noun, signifying *descended, existed, He was,
To Breathe, To Blow,* SUBSTANCE ; to which the letter Yod
gives a distinct visible personality, distinctly defining the
person of Jehovah to be a distinct substantial being of
Substance, who is Eternal and yet can be seen, known, and
felt, in whose person, form, and similitude אלהים, Ehlohim,
can alone be seen as the One true, living, Eternal, Ehlohim
or God ; this is the mystery of the name Jehovah and its
distinction from the name Ehlohim, for while God, the
Eternal Father, is invisible in Himself, He is visible in the
person of Jehovah ; hence the surprise and wonder of
Jacob and Manoah when they declared that they had seen
Ehlohim in the divine person that appeared to them ; and
this personality of Jehovah is supported by the whole of the
Scriptures, wherein Jehovah is invariably recorded as the
divine speaker or medium of communication, and in every
instance where it is written, " Thus saith Jehovah," or as
translated, " Thus saith the LORD." It is *never* Thus saith
Ehlohim, otherwise than in the person of Jehovah or
Jehovah Ehlohim, Messenger Jehovah or Messenger
Ehlohim. Wherever the word GOD occurs in small capitals
accompained by Lord, thus, Lord GOD, as in Gen. xv. 8,
and throughout the book of Ezekiel, &c., it is always a
translation of אדני יהוה, *Lord Jehovah*, where the name
Jehovah is printed with the vowels of Ehlohim : whether
this emanated from Massoretic superstition, or with a view
to conceal the ancient pronunciation, for the present I leave
for our Jewish brethren to determine.

It is clearly recorded that the holy, unchangeable
Ehlohim cannot repent, while the visible substance of
Jehovah both repented and felt grief of heart before He
assumed our nature. Now, why should dust and ashes
dispute with God as to the possibility of such circumstances,
with whom all things are possible ? Who by searching can
find out God, what is His name, and what is His Son's
name ? Abraham called the name of the place upon the
summit of Mount Moriah, יראה יהוה, Jehovah-jireh, *i.e.*,
JEHOVAH WILL BE SEEN, or *Jehovah will appear* (*vide*
margin).

SECTION VI.

THE NEW REVELATION.

In the fourth sermon the Chief Rabbi says: "Now I boldly challenge every professor of the Christian faith to tell me where it is stated that the Prophet, like unto Moses, was to declare a new revelation. On the contrary, the Law given on Sinai is here distinctly declared to be the standard of the truth or falsehood of every future prophet." The holy and inspired language of the unchangeable Law, the prophets, and the holy writings answer this challenge by their own testimony ; for such a challenge only contributes the most invincible proof of their veracity by convicting the man out of his own mouth who put it forth for the fulfilment of Isaiah vi. 8, 9, as expressed in the Jewish translation of Isaac Leeser, patronized by the Jewish association for the diffusion of religious knowledge, and considered by them to be an orthodox impartial (?) translation : "Go, and say unto this people, Hear indeed, but understand not ; and see indeed, but know not. Obdurate will remain the heart of this people, and their ears will be heavy, and their eyes will be shut, so that they will not see with their eyes, nor hear with their ears, nor their hearts be understanding, so that they be converted, and healing be granted them." Compare this with the new covenant declared in Jer. xxxi. 31 —33, in which the ordinances referred to in verse 36 have been continued up to the present day, and are spreading with the increase of Messiah's government as the waters cover the sea, and unto whom the nations of the earth are turning. This is the new revelation or new dispensation spoken of by Jeremiah and prophesied by Moses himself: "A Prophet from the midst of thee, of thy brethren, like unto me, will the Lord thy God raise up unto thee ; unto Him shall ye hearken " (Deut. xviii. 15).

The new revelation is the end of the *ceremonial* Law, by the fulfilment of all that was set forth by its types and shadows by Him who magnified it and made it honourable and satisfied all its demands spoken of by Daniel (ix. 24—27). Thus the new revelation was not to put away the Law, but to establish the honour of the old revelation, by keeping it, inasmuch as it was out of man's power to keep it honourably, perfectly, and disinterestedly, after sin entered the world. Where is the law to be found so plainly written as upon the heart of a believer, though, free from all its demands, he is constrained to delight in its dictates: "Behold, the days come, saith the Lord, that I will make a new covenant with the house of Israel, and with the house of Judah. Not according to the covenant that I made with their fathers in the day that I took them by the hand to bring them out of the land of Egypt; which my covenant they break, although I was an husband unto them, saith the Lord. But this shall be the covenant that I will make with the house of Israel. After those days, saith the Lord, I will put my Law in their inward parts, and write it in their hearts, and will be their God, and they shall be my people" (Jer. xxxi. 31—33). " I am sought of them that asked not for me: I said, Behold me, unto *a nation that was not called by my name*" (Isaiah lxv. 1). I will conclude this reply to the Chief Rabbi's challenge by proving that Moses was a breaker of the law, and incapable of magnifying it and making it honourable.

It is declared in the Scriptures that God told Moses that he had rebelled against Him upon one occasion (Numbers xxvii. 14), which is thus rendered by Leeser, "Because ye rebelled against my order in the desert of Zin," &c. ; and in Psalm cvi. 33, it is stated that " He spoke thoughtlessly with his lips," for which sin Moses was prohibited from entering Canaan. This proves that Moses was a sinner and a law-breaker, who sinned from his own free will; but not to take any undue advantage of this one act under such great provocation and extenuating circumstances (humanly speaking): no doubt Moses had bitterly repented of it, therefore, unregenerate men may regard it as only *a little sin;* but if we contrast the sin of Moses with the sin of Adam, in eating the forbidden fruit at the instigation of his wife, the difficulty would be to determine which was the *smallest sin.* These facts are recorded to prove that any act of disobedience is sin ; therefore, Moses did not magnify the Law and make it honourable, but, on the contrary, he broke the Law by what God declares to be rebellion (Num. xxvii. 14); nor was the Law made honourable at the time Isaiah wrote, as Leeser renders it, " The

Lord willed (to do this) for the sake of His righteousness, (therefore) He magnifieth the Law, and maketh it honourable" (Isaiah xlii. 21). The Jews cannot obliterate the fact that it is the Lord Jehovah Himself who magnifieth the Law and maketh it honourable, and not Moses, as plainly declared by the rendering of Leeser's Bible. Then, if the Lord maketh it honourable and magnifieth it, it must be under the new covenant, spoken of by Jeremiah (xxxi. 31—33). Now, let it be observed that Messiah most positively told His disciples not to think He had come to destroy the Law, but to fulfil the Law and the prophets, declaring the heaven and earth should pass away before the smallest letter of the Law could fail (Matt. v. 17, 18). For the fulfilment of the New Testament predictions, there are almost numberless sects that claim the title of Christians, whose conduct no more proves it than Solomon could prove his righteousness in serving Ashtoreth, Milcom, and Chemosh in his old age (1 Kings xi.)—the same Solomon who wrote, "Train up a child in the way he should go, and when he is old he will not depart from it" (Prov. xxii. 6). Therefore, the new revelation acknowledges the Law to be the only standard of truth that shall endure for ever.

SECTION VII.

POLYTHEISM IN IDOLATRY PROPAGATED BY JEWISH REPRESENTATIONS OF THE TRINITY BEFORE THE CHRISTIAN ERA.

It is well known that many of the heathen idols used in many parts of the East are represented with three heads upon one body as objects of worship, the origin of which can be traced for centuries before the Christian era, which, no doubt, was the result of the iniquitous example of the base and most degraded idolatry of the ten revolted tribes of Israel, who, unable to receive the mystery of the Shemang, declaring the oneness and undivided unity of Ehlohim in Jehovah, were left to the imaginations of their own carnal reason, and so spread their heathenish conception of the One Triune God of Israel among the nations of the earth. Whenever Israel forsook the One Eternal

Jehovah, they were never content with serving but *one image* of wood or stone. It is recorded that Solomon, the wisest man that ever existed, went after *Molech* (1), *Chemosh* (2), and *Milcom* (3) (1 Kings xi. 5, 7, 8), THREE strange gods, and the goddess Ashtoreth. The very next thing that took place was the revolt of the ten tribes from Rehoboam, Solomon's son (1 Kings xii. 20—24), and they have ceased to be a distinct people ever since, except for heathenism and idolatry, wherever any traces are discovered of their observance of the ceremonies of their forefathers: and it is worthy of note that many of the nations and tribes of the East—for instance, in many parts of India—circumcision is still practised among those who serve three-headed idols, with three heads united upon one body, and in other instances three figures upon three equal thrones or elevations, together with many traces of Israelitish idolatry, which has evidently been spread over the face of the earth from the idolatry and evil example of Israel.

SECTION VIII.

JEHOVAH SEEN FACE TO FACE.

GOD told Moses that no man should see His face and live, yet in the very same chapter it is recorded that the Lord spake to Moses face to face, as a man speaketh unto his friend (Exod. xxxiii. 11, 20); therefore it is quite evident that Moses and the patriarchs saw the face of God through some medium. Without recapitulating the facts of Abraham, Hagar, Isaac, and Moses having declared that in Messenger Jehovah or Messenger Ehlohim they beheld Jehovah face to face, the case of Jacob will suffice: "And Jacob called the name of the place פְּנִיאֵל, *Peniel* (God's face), for רָאִיתִי, I have seen, אֱלֹהִים, (Ehlohim) God, פָּנִים אֶל פָּנִים, face to face, and נַפְשִׁי, my life is preserved" (Gen. xxxii. 30). This is rendered strictly according to its literal reading in the Authorized Anglican Version, because the Hebrew root נֶפֶשׁ is used in the Scriptures to denote the natural body or carcase, as may be seen by its

employment in Lev. xxi. 11; Numb. ix. 6, 10, xix. 11,
&c. Wherever it is used it will be found to denote the
natural body, or growth that is developed by blood, and
this is the word used to express the life of Jacob that was
preserved after he had seen God, proving the superior
accuracy of the Authorized Version. The Jewish translation of Dr. Benisch renders it thus :' 'And Jacob called
the name of the place Peniel: for I have seen an *angel*
face to face, and my *soul* is preserved." This is exactly as
it is paraphrased in the Targum of Onkelos, while Isaac
Leeser renders it : "I have seen an *angel of* God face to
face, and my life hath been preserved." These renderings
are by men who venture to state that they are perfectly
impartial translations. Such men vituperate the use of an
article in our version as a crime, while they can delibe-
rately substitute one noun for another, as if it was pur-
posely to keep their own people in ignorance.

Jacob declares he saw the holy, self-existent being of
God face to face in the person of that אִישׁ, man, and, that
there might be no mistake in its commemoration, he called
the name of the place Peniel, which is *the face of God;*
while Jehovah declared that no man should see His face and
live; and, by way of confirmation, God declares by the
prophet Hosea that Jacob had power over Messenger,
"And made supplication unto Him: he found Him in Bethel,
and there he (Jacob) spake עִמָּנוּ, WITH US; even the Lord
God of hosts, who is Jacob's memorial," and witness of
this fact (Hosea xii. 4, 5). This is established and proved
by a multiplicity of passages, but the Law declares two or
three witnesses are sufficient : compare Gen. xxxii. 28, 30,
xlviii. 16; 1 Kings xviii. 31; Hosea xii. 4, 5.

The rendering of this last passage in Isaac Leeser's
Jewish translation proves how severely the death-knell
sounded by the twelfth chapter of Hosea against the
doctrines of Judaism is felt by the Jews, because this
translator has taken upon himself to break the law (Deut.
iv. 2) by adding the numeral adjective ONE, notwith-
standing the absence of this word, אֶחָד, in the Hebrew text,
unconscious of the fact that such an interpolation only tends
to confirm the doctrine of the Shemang, namely, that עִמָּנוּ,
with US, includes Messenger Jehovah in אֶחָד, one unity,
confirming that our plural Ehlohim is one by an Eternal
unity. Now compare this with the author's statement in the

preface, in which he states that he has "thrown aside all bias "—"no perversion or forced rendering of *any text* was needed to bear out his opinions or those of Israelites in general; and he for one would place but little confidence in them, if he were compelled to change the evident meaning of the Bible to find a support for them." Now compare this translator's rendering of Hos. xii. 4, 5, 6, with his own preface and his rendering of Deut. iv. 2.

All these apparently contradictory passages are at once reconciled by faith in the divine mystery of the Trinity, because there are passages to prove that they are not figurative expressions used in those passages, where it is recorded that Jehovah has an arm, hands, feet, face, heart, breath, mouth, eyes, ears, nose, &c., representing a distinct form and similitude, in the likeness and image of which He created man, saying, "Let us make man in our צלם, CROSS, or image:" this root, according to Talmudical language (*vide* Bresslau's Heb. Lexicon) signifies a cross, as shown by the form of a man with his arms extended. A striking illustration of this is given by the victory of the Iraelites over the Amalekites, when the Lawgiver Moses had his arms raised by *the high priest*, giving him the form of a cross and the prevalency of Amalek when he failed to extend his arms in this form or attitude (Exodus xvii. 11, 12). The objection of the Jews to admit that Jehovah has a form and similitude is answered by Moses, who has recorded the reason why the Israelites were not permitted to see the form and similitude of Jehovah, *i.e.*, because they were a stiff-necked obstinate people, prone to the most gross and depraved idolatry (Exodus xxxii., xxxiii). Therefore, they were not permitted to see Jehovah, "Lest ye corrupt yourselves, and make you a graven image, the similitude of any figure," &c., &c. (Deut. iv. 12—19). So prone were the children of Israel to the most revolting idolatry that if it had not been for the faithfulness, long-suffering, and mercy of Jehovah, for the sake of His oath and covenant with Abraham, Isaac, and Jacob, no traces of them would have existed at the present time (Ezek. xxxvi. 22). When Moses talked with Jehovah face to face, as a man speaketh with his friend, the Eternal occupied an enclosed space of two cubits and a half by one cubit and a half wide, covered by the wings of the cherubims meeting

over the top of the mercy seat of the Ark of the testimony
made by Bezaleel (Exodus xxxvii. 6). The prophet
Isaiah, in spirit, speaking by the dictation of Jehovah,
records the reason why these things are חחד from the
eyes of unbelievers : "I heard the voice of the Eternal
saying, Whom shall I send, and who will go, לנו, for US?"
Jehovah the Eternal Son answers, "Then said I, Here (am)
I ; send me. And He (the Eternal) said Go, and tell this
people, Hear ye indeed, but understand not; and see ye
indeed, but perceive not. Make the heart of this people fat,
and make their ears heavy, and shut their eyes ; lest they
see with their eyes, and hear with their ears, and understand with their heart, and convert, and be healed"
(Isaiah vi. 8—10). This proves that Jehovah the Eternal
Son, under *a covenant of works, is the destroying Angel of that
covenant,* which He could, in justice to its holy demands,
only establish, magnify, and make it honourable by fulfill-
ing it Himself, for the vindication of its honour and glory,
and for the establishment of the new covenant of justifica-
tion by faith in the Eternal Son of God, who declares, "I
have not spoken in secret from the beginning; from the
time that it was, there am I (*i.e.*, Jehovah the Eternal Son):
and now the Lord God, and His Spirit, hath sent ME"
(Isaiah xlviii. 16). If this is not the language of the
Eternal Son of God, it certainly was not the language of
Isaiah, who was not from the BEGINNING, nor from
the time that it was (or more literally מעת היותה שם אני,
from before time there I), because Moses wrote before
Isaiah, and he does not tell us that Isaiah was from
the beginning ; but that Ehlohim was the Creator of the
Heavens and the Earth in the beginning. The sense
of what Isaiah writes is this, I have not spoken in secret
from the beginning; before time had existence there
I AM, and now the Lord God and His Spirit hath sent
me ; that is, the person who here speaks declares that He
has not spoken in secret, but that He was in the beginning,
before time was He existed. "What is, שם־בנו, His
SON'S name, if thou knowest?" (Prov. xxx. 4). Daniel is
the only inspired writer who mentions Jehovah by His
new covenant name, משיח, Messiah. When Nebuchad-
nezzar declared that he saw four men walking loose in the
midst of the burning fiery furnace, he said the form of the
fourth is like בר אלהין, (Chaldee for) the SON of God, whom

he afterwards called the most High God, which Shadrach,
Meshach, and Abednego did not contradict. Yet the Jews
render this thus, "And the appearance of the fourth is
like a son of the gods ;" evidently unmindful that by their
denial of the fact that the King of Babylon really and
truly beheld Jehovah the Eternal Son, referred to in
Prov. xxx. 4, they thereby acknowledge an equal power
of deliverance by the agency of false gods ; for not a
hair was singed, nor had the smell of fire passed upon
the three Hebrews, while it consumed those who cast them
into the fiery furnace.

SECTION IX.

THE BRAZEN SERPENT AND THE SECOND COMMANDMENT.

If the divine personality of the Word as Messenger Jehovah be obliterated from the Scriptures, it must neces-
sarily follow that such persons who attempt this must
thereby charge Jehovah with sanctioning idolatry, by
commanding Moses to make a BRAZEN SERPENT for
the people to look at, *instead* of looking to Jehovah for a
cure. Now we know the brazen serpent was a GRAVEN
IMAGE in the LIKENESS of a thing that creeps in the
earth and under the earth, to which Jehovah commanded
Israel to look for a cure, instead of Himself; for the
people had prayed to the Eternal for the fiery flying
serpents to be taken away, but He would not deliver
them till they had looked at the image of the serpent of
brass, or copper, as rendered by the Jews : "And Moses
made a serpent of copper, and put it upon a pole : and it
came to pass, that when a serpent had bitten any man, and
he looked up to the serpent of copper, he remained alive"
(Numbers xxi. 9, Leeser's Bible). Now, if this does not
bear witness of Him who was made sin, and in the likeness of sinful flesh, and numbered with the transgressors,
He who magnified the Law and made it honourable (Isaiah
liii.), not to put away the Law, but to fulfil it (Isaiah xlii.
21), for the establishment of the New Covenant (Jer. xxxi.
31—33), what can such circumstances contribute to vindicate the honour of the first commandment, written by the

c

FINGER of Jehovah, who had no manner of form, image,
nor similitude (to say nothing of fingers, &c.) but that of
the Angel of His presence? "Thou shalt have no other
gods (Ehlohim) before me. Thou shalt not make unto thyself any GRAVEN IMAGE or any likeness of anything that
is in the heaven above, or that is in the earth beneath, or
that is in the water under the earth," &c., &c. (Exod. xx.
3, 4). What becomes of the truth of the Scriptures in this
case without Jehovah Jah, the Eternal Son of God? because
any attempt to obliterate the doctrine of the vicarious
atonement of the Son of God is to charge Him with sanctioning idolatry, while there is no sin recorded beside
that of unbelief He hates more than idolatry.

SECTION X.

JEHOVAH REPENTING.

THERE are many passages of the Scriptures where it is
recorded that Jehovah repented, as in Exod. xxxii. 14;
2 Sam. xxiv. 16; Judges ii. 18; 1 Sam. xv. 35; 1 Chron.
xxi. 15; Jer. xxvi. 19; Psalm cvi. 45; Amos vii. 3; Jonah
iii. 10: but the most remarkable passage is in Gen. vi.
6, 7: "And it repented the Lord that He had made man
on the earth, and it grieved Him at His heart." And the
cause of His so repenting is recorded to be in consequence
of the wicked and degraded condition of man, because
"every imagination of the thoughts of his heart was only
evil continually" (ver. 5). Therefore we have not far to
go to ascertain the effect of sin in the sight of Jehovah,
since it is recorded that it "grieved Him at His heart," or,
as Dr. Benisch renders it, 'It pained His heart.' Yet in
another passage it is written, אלהים, Ehlohim "is not a
man that He should lie; neither the son of man that He
should repent: hath He not said, and shall He not do it? or
hath He spoken, and shall He not make it good" (Numb.
xxiii. 19). These words were uttered by Balaam, of whom
it is recorded that he (Balaam) spake against his own inclina-
tion by the dictation of God, without the power of reversing
the blessing of God. Now the same word used in these

passages to express repentance is used in Jer. viii. 6: "No
man repented him of his wickedness." What are we to
infer from this but a most glaring contradiction? because
in one place it states that "God is not a man that He
should lie; neither the son of man that He should repent;"
and in other places it is written that Jehovah did repent,
so much so that it "grieved Him at His heart." Let it be
carefully observed that Ehlohim, the One Triune God, is a
word that is not used when it is recorded that *the Lord
repented;* but the word Jehovah, יהוה, is the divine
person that is represented as repenting, and never אלהים,
Ehlohim. This proves that it is only one divine person of
the undivided Trinity that is represented as the subject of
repentance and grief, and in no case the Trinity of persons
as expressed by *Ehlohim,** unless prefixed by the definite
article defining the person of the Mediator to be Ehlohim. Compare Gen. xxii. 1, with verses 12, 15—18, and
Exod. iii., where the angel claims the title of God and
Jehovah. The Targum of Onkelos endeavours to reconcile
this by admitting the divine personality of the Word, thus:
"And it repented the Lord in His Word that He had made
men upon the earth;" and in the next verse it is paraphrased, "because it repenteth me in my Word that I
have made them." A similar reading is given in the Targums of Palestine and Jonathan of Jerusalem.

Jehovah is not called the son of man till after he came
down from heaven and assumed our nature, by being born
of a woman and dwelling among us, עמנואל, *Emmanuel,*
"God with us" (Isaiah vii. 14—16). Therefore is it clear
that Jehovah, who repented and was grieved and pained
at His heart, was the identical person of the Eternal Son
of God, called the Word of the Lord,—דבר־יהוה, *Jehovah
Dovor*—(1 Kings xviii. 31), in whom Jacob saw Ehlohim face
to face (Gen. xxxii.); and Jehovah declares He is Jacob's
Memorial (Hos. xii.). This divine person of the Eternal Word
is revealed to be Jehovah, who was grieved at His heart and
smitten of Ehlohim, with whom He was One, who put him
to grief, and numbered Him with transgressors, so that the
existence of sin has been the cause of grief, pain, and sorrow
to Jehovah the Eternal Son of God ever since sin came into

---

* I am not aware that this distinction in the employment of the names
Jehovah and Ehlohim has ever been pointed out before, or noticed by any
writer whatever.

existence; but, for the sake of His covenant and oath, He has mercifully been pleased to bear with it. Now comes the question suggested by the carnal reason of our desperately wicked hearts (Jer. xvii. 9), How could Jehovah repent in His divine person? Such a question proves the devilish depravity of our hearts by the development of that pretension to discern between good and evil we inherit in our hearts and nature from the disobedience of our forefather Adam, when he rebelled against God by robbing Him of the knowledge of good and evil. "In all their affliction HE (Jehovah) *was afflicted*" (Isa. lxiii. 9). It should be sufficient for us to know that it is revealed to us that it was not the Triune Ehlohim who repented, and felt grief of heart, but the divine person of Jehovah, who declares in Jer. xv. 6: "Thou hast forsaken me, saith JEHOVAH, thou art gone backward: therefore will I stretch out my hand against thee, and destroy thee; I AM WEARY OF REPENTING." Here another suggestion from our sin-contaminated knowledge of good and evil objects, because it cannot comprehend how the divine person of Jehovah could have a heart or any form, image, similitude, or likeness before He took our human nature upon Him—that is no business of ours, any more than the reason why Jehovah would not tell His name to Jacob when he wrestled with Him, or when He appeared to Manoah, is anything to do with us. We cannot comprehend the divine mystery of the Trinity, who created man in the form, image, and likeness of Ehlohim. It was in the form of a man Ehlohim wrestled with Jacob, appeared to Hagar, Manoah, and Moses. Jehovah was personified by three men when He appeared to Abraham, and whom Abraham addressed as One person, and who was seen to be personally present walking about among the glowing coals of the burning fiery furnace with the three Hebrews. We should be ever mindful that all things are possible with God, and that there is nothing impossible with Him, and that it is the development of our sinful knowledge of good and evil, to speculate upon the possibility of any of His actions, dispensations, or anything that He has revealed, concerning which we have *no right to give an opinion*, but to receive and believe His most holy word without questioning it; for who by searching can find out God? Who can find out the Almighty unto perfection? (Job xi. 7) "The secret things belong unto the

Lord our Ehlohim: but those things which are revealed belong unto us and to our children for ever, that we may do all the words of this law " (Deut xxix. 29). Therefore if we obliterate the revelation of the divine personality of the Word, and all the evidences of the Trinity, what dependence could be placed upon Him? He would be liable to repent and change His mind. But if we are able to discern Jehovah as repenting and feeling grieved, in consequence of His being put to grief as the Eternal Son and servant of the Father (Isaiah xlii.), we shall vindicate the truth of the Scripture by the reconciliati n of what must otherwise constitute the most apparent contradiction : " Behold my servant, whom I uphold ; mine elect, in whom my soul delighteth ; I have put my spirit upon Him : He shall bring forth judgment to the Gentiles " (Isaiah xlii. 1). In the fifth verse (אל, El) God, by the singular form of the noun, declares that He is this same Jehovah who created the heavens and spread forth the earth. In ch. xxvi. 4, it is written, " Trust ye in Jehovah, because in JAH Jehovah is the Rock of Ages " (*ride* margin) ; or it may be read *with* JAH, Jehovah is the Rock of Ages, or everlasting strength. Job believed this ; hence it is written, " For I know that my Redeemer liveth, and that He shall stand at the latter day upon the earth " (Job xix. 25). " Who shall declare His way to His face ? and who shall repay Him what He hath done ? Yet shall HE be brought to the GRAVE, and shall remain in the tomb " (Job xxi. 31, 32 —33, 34). The Jews render these passages thus : " And well I know that my Redeemer liveth, and that He will remain as the last after the creatures of the dust (are passed away)." " (But) who will tell Him to His face of His way ? and who will repay Him what He hath done ? Yea, HE will indeed be CARRIED to the GRAVE, and men will quickly think of His monument." " The clods of the valley shall be sweet unto Him, and every man shall draw after Him, as there are innumerable before Him " (ver. 33).

SECTION XI.

" I will declare the decree : the Lord hath said unto me, Thou art
my Son, this day have I begotten thee."—PSALM ii. 7.

THIS is a prophetic revelation made by the divine person
of the Eternal Son of God concerning His incarnation ;
here is the declaration to men by the witness of the Trinity
that He was and is the Eternal Son of God in His divine
person, followed by the declaration of the decree concerning the time of His manifestation in the body prepared
for Him. Man's idea of God's expression of time is no
point of consideration with God, as scholars are well acquainted with the fact that in the inspired writings of the
Hebrew Scriptures the preterit (perfect or past) tense is
often used for the future tense, according to man's vocabulary
and understanding; for an instance, *vide* Leeser's rendering of Exod. iii. 14, אהיה אשר אהיה, " I will be
that I will be ; " Authorized Version, "I AM THAT I AM."
The primary and radical meaning of the Hebrew root,
בנה, from which the word *Son* is derived signifies *to build ;*
hence its derivatory signification of near relationship.
When applied to the Son of God, as in Prov. xxx. 4, it
has no reference to preceding or succeeding existence ; the
question is one, " What is His name, and what is His Son's
name, if thou canst tell ? " Its etymology defines a relationship from the *similarity and likeness of one to another*,
also one who is between, as a representative or Mediator,
hence בין, *between ;* or, from the adaptation of one thing to
another, without the slightest reference to time or date of
existence in either case beyond what men infer from the
circumstances of its employment: for instance, when men are
called the sons or children of men in the Bible, it refers to their
similarity one to another collectively, as one man resembles
another; and as man is adapted for the society of his fellow
creatures, so the Son of God is Eternal like the Father, and
is adapted for His society; and, again, in a metaphorical sense,
as the stones of a building are related to and adapted to one
another in form, position, and similarity, as expressed by
the root from which the word בן, son, is derived, hence
it is used of families, as the building up of the house,

(Ruth iv. 11; Deut. xxv. 9), and in Gen. ii. 22, its employment is remarkably significant: "And the rib which
the Lord God had taken from man, רִיבֶן, BUILDED He a
woman" (vide the marginal reading); and man recognized
the woman as a part of himself, being a portion of his own
body that was with him when God first created him, and
the man and the woman were one flesh. This is a striking
figure of the unity of Ehlohim in Jehovah: here the same
word or root from which *son* is derived is used to convey
the idea of building as its primary and radical signification,
setting forth the Eternal Son of God to be the eternal
foundation and Rock of Ages upon which His Church is
built, whose person is the principal theme of the Psalms,
and to whom many of them are expressly dedicated, as the
Chief Musician of the Church, by the inspired pen of David,
the sweet Psalmist of Israel, who, by the inspiration of the
Holy Spirit, describes the sufferings and persecution of
Messiah, particularly in those Psalms dedicated to the
Eternal Son of God as the Chief Musician: see also those
written for the service of the Sanctuary, to be sung by
those singers termed the Sons of Korah: "The stone
which the builders refused is become the head stone of the
corner" (Psalm cxviii. 22).

The employment of the word *son* to distinguish objects
that are adapted one to another is an idiom peculiar to the
Hebrew; an arrow is termed the *son of a bow*, a twig or
branch is called the *son of a tree*, &c. All these circumstances prove that when God uses the term son, He uses it
without reference to time: "Thou art my Son;" and in
Exod. iv. 22, "Thus saith Jehovah, Israel is my son, even
my firstborn." This does not exclude Abraham and Isaac,
the father and grandfather of Israel, from the same privi-
lege. A man is said to be the son of man because he is
like man: so far as the term is concerned, it refers exclusively
to physical similitude and likeness, and mentally to similarity of mind, pursuits, and habits—a creature of time,
subject to disease, trouble, sin, and death; so Jehovah is the
Son of God because He is like God in purity and holiness;
not a creature of time, but eternal—really and truly the
Eternal Son of God. Let it be observed that the divine
person alluded to in the second Psalm is declared to be the
Son who was acknowledged by the Trinity as the Eternal
Son in His divine person *before* He declared the decree

relating to His incarnation. This is the first written declaration revealing the f.ct that the divine person of the Eternal Word,—דבר־יהוה, *Jehovah Dovor* (1 Kings xviii. 31; Gen. xxxii.)—Messenger Jehovah, and Messenger Elhohim, the medium of communication between God and man —was really and truly the Eternal Son of God, testifying " this day, ילדתיך, have I begotten Thee," or *brought Thee forth, i.e.*, brought Thee forth to the recognition of the nations of the earth, having prophetic reference to the definite time or day of His incarnation. Therefore the term begotten, when applied to the Son of God, admits of no reference or inference whatever to time or date of existence, but exclusively to similarity of being, *i.e.*, the express image, person, similitude, and representative of the Father, as proved by the language of the Trinity addressed to the then existing Eternal person of the Son of God : " Thou art my Son ; this day have I begotten thee ;" not implying origin or date of existence, but of the open manifestation of Him who rent the vail of the temple, whose goings forth were from all eternity (Micah v. 2), as a distinct person in the Trinity of the Godhead, throwing open the Holy of Holies that typified His previous obscurity in the bosom of the Father under a covenant of works. It is in this passage of Scripture declared for a decree that this medium of communication, who gave the Law through Moses, and spake with him face to face as a man speaketh with his friend, and who appeared to Abraham, Isaac, Jacob, Manoah, and Hagar, is Jehovah the Eternal Son of God, who fulfilled the Law, magnified it, and made it honourable, for the establishment of the new dispensation under the covenant of grace, or unmerited favour (Isa. lxv. 1). To prove that the word ילד (*sent forth*, or) *brought forth*, when applied to Jehovah, has no reference to time, or date, or origin of existence, in the sense placed upon it by the construction instigated by the corrupt imagination of the heart of man, which is only evil continually (Gen. vi. 5 ; Jer. xvii. 9), it is written that God revealed the fact that He was His Eternal Son : " The Lord said unto ME, Thou art my Son "—the eternally then existing eternal ME, I, and HE, before this prophetic revelation of His incarnation, the same Eternal Son (Messenger Jehovah), who declared Isaac to be the *only son* of Abraham, while Abraham actually had another son named Ishmael, thirteen years older than Isaac, living at the same time that Elhohim declared Isaac to be Abraham's *only* son; and though Abraham loved his son Ishmael (Gen. xxi. 10, 11), who was as much his son as Dan and Naphtali, Gad and Asher, were the sons of Jacob by his concubines Bilah and Zilpah. Carnal reason objects, If Messiah is the Eternal Son of God spoken of in Prov. xxx. 4, how can He be the begotten Son of God? Faith replies, With God all things are possible, particularly those things which are impossible with men, and *contrary to reason*. God plainly declares, "Thou art my Son"—a declaration of His eternal similitude to the Eternal Father—His representative and medium of communication, the same divine and distinct Eternal Son who declares in Isaiah xlv. 21, "I am a just God and a Saviour." How could three men walk loose in the midst of the glowing coals of a burning fiery furnace without being consumed? Because the Eternal Son of God was with them before He was manifest in the flesh. The root of the word Saviour, יש, in Isaiah xlv. 21, is used to express the name Joshua, which is the Hebrew name for *Jesus*, and is rendered Ἰησους, Jesus, in the translation called the Septuagint, made by the seventy-two Jews nearly three hundred years before the coming of Messiah; therefore, as the meaning of the name Jesus or Joshua signifies a *Saviour* in both Greek and Hebrew, it is not inconsistent to read, *I am a just God and a Jesus;* but, more literally, I am a just God and a Saviour, or one who delivers and makes free from every claim, from every demand and every punishment, *i.e.*, a mighty and matchless Saviour when applied to God. Consequently, when God uses the words *only Son* and *begotten*, it can only be the development of sin for sinful, finite, human creatures to attempt to place any construction upon the word of God, to pretend to understand the language of infinite holiness and purity. God declares that He had anointed and strengthened Cyrus to subdue nations before him, though Cyrus was not born till 113 years after this declaration (Isaiah xlv. 1); nor was it fulfilled till 176 years afterwards, when Cyrus was sixty-three years of age; yet it is spoken of as an accomplished fact 176 years before men witnessed its fulfilment. Compare Isaiah xlv. 1; 2 Chron. xxxvi. 21—23; Ezra i. 1. How repeatedly and urgently the Eternal Son of God, as the divine person of the Word or medium of communication,

declares that He is really and truly God, who will not give
His glory to another: "Remember the former things of
old: for I am God, and there is none else; I am God,
and there is none like ME, declaring the end from the
beginning, and from ancient times the things that are not
yet done," &c. (Isaiah xlvi. 9, 10). The Chief Rabbi
quibbles with the word *Son* in Psalm ii. 12, in consequence of
its being the Chaldee word *Bar*, בַּר; but he does not explain
why the same word is used for *Son* in the Targums. The
Jewish translation of Leeser renders this verse, "Do
homage to the Son, lest He be angry, and ye be lost on
the way; for His wrath is so speedily kindled. Happy
are all they that put their trust in Him."

The Chief Rabbi takes upon himself the responsibility of
rendering the words יִרְאֶה זֶרַע, in Isaiah liii. 10, thus: "He
shall see His seed," by inserting the pronoun *his* as if it
occurred in the text, without distinguishing the interpolation of this word by italics, to denote that the pronominal
suffix does not occur in the original: for proof see Isaac
Leeser's rendering of this passage, where the pronoun *His*
is inserted in a parenthesis, and also the Authorized Version,
where it is faithfully denoted by italics. Not content with
this, the Chief Rabbi remarks upon his own misrepresenta-
tion as follows: "This signifies that the servant of the
Lord should leave an offspring. The Nazarene, however,
is said to have died childless." Such statements as these,
contradicted as they are by his own authorities, can only
have a tendency to very materially detract from that respect
that is justly due to those who endeavour to consistently
maintain and support those convictions they believe to be
true. The word זֶרַע, "seed," as it stands in Isaiah liii. 10,
cannot imply any such inference as this author maintains,
because for "His seed" it would stand thus, זַרְעוֹ, as in
Gen. xlvi. 6, 7, &c.; therefore no just inference can be made
that the Nazarene should leave children or an offspring as
understood by carnal-minded men: the seed that He should
see were the spiritual children of the Most High (Psalm
lxxii. 6)—taken one of a city and two of a family (Jer. iii.
14, 15). This is the increase of His government He should
see as the *travail of His soul*. Nothing carnal is hinted at;
otherwise, how can the carnal mind of man understand by
the natural understanding the endless increase of Messiah's
government by the choice of *one* of a city and *two* of a family?

If it be contended that the words "This day have I begotten Thee" refer to a supposed date of His *Sonship*, as understood by men, we find the same divine person of the Eternal Son Himself contradicting such a supposition or opinion nearly 350 years afterwards, by the prophet Isaiah. The divine person of the Eternal Son or Jehovah declares, "YEA, BEFORE THE DAY WAS I am HE" (Isa. xliii. 13), *i.e.*, the day spoken of in Psalm ii. 7. That ye may know and believe me, and understand that I am HE: before me there was no God formed, neither shall there be after ME. I, even I, am, יהוה, the HE WILL BE, and beside me there is no (*Jesus*, that is) Saviour, or as rendered, I even I, am Jehovah, and beside me there is no Saviour. I have declared and have saved, and I have showed when there was no strange God among you: therefore ye are my witnesses, saith Jehovah, that I am God; yea, before the day—*i.e.*, before the day of His incarnation, referred to in Psalm ii. 7—I am HE, and there is none that can deliver out of my hand : I will work, and who shall let it ? "Thus saith Jehovah your REDEEMER, the Holy One of Israel, Thou shalt know no God but me; for there is no Saviour beside me" (Hos. xiii. 4); that is, Jehovah is really and truly the divine person of the Eternal Son of God—"What is his Son's name, if thou canst tell ?" (Prov. xxx. 4)—HE who in after day took our nature upon Him, and was manifest in the flesh as Immanuel, God with us, Jehovah our righteousness, the Messenger whose goings forth have been from of old, from everlasting, or from the days of eternity (Mic. v. 2)—the Messenger of the Covenant, THE LORD HIMSELF, who came suddenly to His temple (the temple of His human body) (Mal. iii. 1 ; Mic. v. 2). This proves that Jehovah was eternally the divine *person* or *substance* of the Son of God before His incarnation, and that the words "This day have I begotten Thee" have a prophetic reference to the temple of His body prepared for Him through the line of Judah, the stem of Jesse, and the Son of David. "And it shall be at *that day*, saith Jehovah, thou shalt call ME *my* MAN ; and shalt call me no more *my* Lord" (Hos. ii. 16 ; verse 18 in Hebrew Bible and Leeser's translation). Here the person of Jehovah declares a given definite time when HE Jehovah Himself shall be called *man* instead of Lord, that is, our equal as a brother and fellow-man : compare this word אישי, Ishi, *my man*, with the root אִישׁ, Ish, *man*, in the marginal reading of Gen. ii. 23, also in Leeser's translation : the noun אִישׁ, Ish, being always used to denote human nature, and is the root of the words *man, woman, husband*, and *wife*. In the previous chapter the Lord had declared that HE will no more have mercy upon the house of Israel, because He would utterly take them away (Hos. i. 6). Has not this been fulfilled by the coming of the Eternal Son, to whom the Father said, "Ask of me, and I will give Thee the גוים, nations, for Thine inheritance, and the uttermost parts of the earth for Thy possession " (Psalm ii. 8). To which the Chief Rabbi objects, "Now, if the Son be a Divinity like the Father, and equal to Him, why need He ask that any favours should be granted Him ? Is He not omnipotent ? Is not the whole earth with the fulness thereof His possession ?" This question is answered by the fact that Jehovah took upon Himself the human nature of man, the form of a servant, that His OBEDIENCE and righteousness might be imputed to all who are enabled to believe in Him ; He made His soul an offering for sin. " Blessed is the man unto whom the Lord imputeth not iniquity," &c. (Psalm xxxii. 2). For in the sight of God "shall no man living be justified" (Psalm cxliii. 2 ; Job xv. 14, xxv. 4 ; Eccles. vii. 20).

SECTION XII.

THE WONDERFUL WORD "JAH."

The name Jehovah is a pure Hebrew word, signifying The Eternal ; it is expressed by four letters, Yod, י, He, ה, Vau, ו, He, ה, thus יהוה, Jehovah. These letters are called the Tetragrammaton, and form the component parts of the past, present, and future tenses, expressing the THREE attributes of eternity, He was, He is, He will be : hence Jehovah is always הוא, HE, and אהיה, I AM, because He can only be like Himself. See Dr. Benisch's translation, Exod. iii. 14, in whose translation Jehovah is always rendered by *The Eternal*.

There is a most remarkable and mysterious name by which Jehovah is occasionally distinguished in the Scrip-

tures as a distinct person, and yet inseparably One in
Jehovah—the name יה, JAH : it occurs forty-nine times in
the Bible, twice in Exodus, forty-three times in the Psalms,
and four times in Isaiah.   It is usually translated in the
same manner as the name Jehovah is rendered, namely,
LORD, in small capitals, and in only one instance it is
rendered in our version as it occurs in the original (Psalm
lxviii. 4), "Sing unto Ehlohim, sing praises to His name :
extol Him that rideth upon the heavens by His name JAH,
and rejoice before Him." In Isaiah xii. 2, it is rendered
Yah by Leeser : "Behold, God is my salvation ; I will trust
and not be afraid; for my strength and song is Yah the
Eternal ; and He is become my salvation ;" and in xxvi. 4,
the same Jewish authority renders it, "Trust ye in the
Lord unto eternity ; for in Yah the Lord is everlasting protection."

Dr. Benisch renders Exod. xvii. 16, thus—"For he said,
Because the hand is upon the throne of Yah, war from the
Eternal with Amalek from generation to generation."   In
Isaiah xxxviii. 11, this word JAH (Yah or Yoh) occurs
twice : "I said I shall not see JAH, JAH in the land of the
living," &c.

Moses sang in his song, "JAH is my strength and song,
He is become my salvation" (Exod. xv. 2). Jah is expressed
by two letters, *Yod*, *He*, which with *Vav*, *He*, form Jehovah ;
and these letters are pronounced by a sound of nature in
the act of respiration or breathing.   It is from these letters
the word יהי, YEHEE, is formed, which is literally *shall be*,
rendered "Let there be," and is fully expressed by the
sound of nature in act of the drawing and escape of one
breath from the lungs; this was the word used by God
that brought the world, the light, and the firmament into
existence, namely, by the sound of *Yehee*,* "Let there be."
It went forth with power, and accomplished the thing
whereunto it was sent without returning unto Him void :
the effect produced was the existence of the world.   How
forcibly this illustrates Psalm xxxiii. 6! "By the word of
the Lord were the heavens made ; and all the host of them
by the breath of His mouth."   "For with Jah the Lord
created the world."

The difference in the rendering of Isaiah xxvi. 4, I
have given in Section IV., from Solomon Lyon's Hebrew

* *Vide* the Hebrew Grammar of Solomon Lyon.

Grammar, may be accounted for by a difference of opinion as to the meaning of the words צוּר עוֹלָמִים, rendered *everlasting strength* or protection (Rock of Ages in the margin); but as the word rendered everlasting is the plural form, this word is used in the Hebrew Bible for *world*, and as the verb צוּר in this verse describes the action of Jehovah by the same word employed in Gen. ii. 7, to form, bind, compress, &c. (*vide* also the Lexicons of Gesenius, Crake, Bagster, &c.), disinterested scholars will doubtless give the preference to the rendering of Solomon Lyon, the Israelite, proving that God, in company with the distinct person of JAH, created the world, and at the same time in such an inexplicable, mysterious, undivided union with Jehovah as to constitute but One and the same Jehovah Ehlohim.

In Isaiah ix. 6, it is written "Unto us a Child is born, unto us a Son is given, whose name shall be called *Wonderful.*" This is recorded in the preterit or past tense, as the facts of a complete and perfect action, from which the Jews maintain that it has reference to Hezekiah, who was born about thirty-nine years before, and therefore cannot refer to Messiah, because the Nazarene did not appear till 740 years after ; whereas such an objection only tends to reflect additional proof of the Eternal Sonship of Messiah, who was Jehovah Himself, the then existing Eternal Son of God, the Son that is given, the Child that was born, whose name is Wonderful, Mighty God, the Eternal Father. The words will admit of no other rendering without doing violence to their employment throughout the whole of the Scriptures. The Chief Rabbi identifies the word אֵל (El), God, in the singular number, as it occurs in this verse, with a mere human hero! But as God employed this word אֵל, El, in the Law to describe Himself as a jealous אֵל, GOD, the Chief Rabbi's definition appears irreverent, since he defines this word to signify a mere hero, by attempting, with Philippson, after the example of Ben Ezra, to show that it points to Hezekiah. (See Notes to Leeser's Bible.)

But according to the Scriptures we behold, not Hezekiah, but Jehovah the Eternal Father, and Jehovah the Eternal Son, the ONE mighty God, in that Child. This is supported by Zech. xiv. 9 : " And Jehovah *was* for a King over all the earth : in THAT DAY shall there be one Jehovah, and his name One." Here is a prophetic reference to a future day, when Jehovah should take human nature into union with Himself, declaring that He would still be but One Jehovah even in THAT DAY. This is according to the Jewish rendering of היה, *was*, instead of "shall be." The Child born and Son given should be no addition to the persons of the Trinity, but that He should still constitute the same undivided unity of one Jehovah, who is three persons in one and the same God. Throughout the Scriptures it will be found, wherever Jehovah uses the words "*In that day*," by applying them to circumstances and events He is about to bring to pass, they will generally be found to point to the day of His humiliation, when He, as the seed of the woman, should bruise the serpent's head (Gen. iii. 15): "In that day Jehovah shall be one, and his name One," *i.e.*, the day when He should be called *man*.

Thus Jehovah proves *His* name to be *Wonderful*. It is rather a pitiable weakness of the Jews to assert that the passage in Isaiah ix. 6, points to Hezekiah as the *Eternal Father, the Mighty God*, while it is recorded that the unchangeable God told Hezekiah after this prophecy that his house, with his sons and children, should be utterly taken away (2 Kings xx. 17, 18). And because of the wickedness of Manasseh, Hezekiah's son, the Lord declared He would wipe Jerusalem as a man wipeth a dish, turning it upside down (2 Kings xxi. 11—13), for the fulfilment of the desolations recorded in the book of Daniel.

What are we to understand by the question of Agur in Prov. xxx. 4,—"What is His name, and what is His SON'S name, if thou canst tell?"—but an immediate reference to the distinct person of JAH by whom God made the worlds (Heb. i. 2)? I refrain from making any dogmatic assertions of my own, because the fact is but too obvious to all those who are disinterestedly jealous for the integrity of the written word of God in preference to the evasions of men.

The Targumists were fully aware of this, and attempted to meet the difficulty by distinguishing the divine personality of Messenger Jehovah, or Messenger Ehlohim, as MEMRA, The Word, as I have already shown, because it is clearly recorded by inspired penmen that in the distinct person of Jah Jehovah is everlasting strength, or the Rock of Ages, clearly conveying that, out of Jah, God is a consuming fire. What is His Son's name? The first letter in the Hebrew word Son is Beth, which signifies a house or place of refuge; and as it is written that Ehlohim in Jehovah is one, we can understand Prov. xviii. 10: "The name of Jehovah is a strong tower: the righteous runneth into it and is safe." It was the mysterious letter ה, HEE, with which Jah is written, and that also expresses the act of breathing in the word Jehovah and YEHEE, *Let there be*, that indicates life, existence, and eternity, that was added or inserted in the names of Abraham and Sarah by the divine person of the Word of the Lord or Messenger Jehovah. It was the pronunciation of this letter as a part of the letter *Shin*, ש, that caused the difficulty to the Ephraimites in their attempts to pronounce SHibboleth, which they could only pronounce with a *Samech*, ס, without the H, thus, Sibboleth (Judges xii. 6), proving that they had no divine life in their language.

I now conclude this part, though it has been with considerable difficulty I have been enabled to condense this pamphlet into its present form; it is the result of careful study of the Holy Scriptures alone, never having read any work or commentary of any description upon the subject, embracing the inspired writings of Moses and the prophets exclusively, for testimony to the revelation of the Trinity in unity of the Godhead. I have not written to support any preconceived sectarian opinion, but in reply to an attack and challenge upon the fundamental doctrine of the Law and the Prophets, that our Jewish brethren may read for themselves. I have endeavoured to act upon the two first principles sanctioned and recognized by the recent synod— (1) individual authority in religious matters; (2) the primary importance of free scientific investigation—reserving the vindication of the righteousness of the third proposition —*i.e.*, the rejection of the belief in Israel's restoration—for the subject of another pamphlet at a future period (D.V.), wherein I shall endeavour to prove the truth of the Scriptures, by showing that those prophecies that are claimed for the temporal restoration of Israel were all fulfilled to the letter by the return from the Babylonish captivity under Ezra and Nehemiah; and the complete fulfilment of Scripture by the coming of Messiah, who will come no more till He comes at the final judgement day; and, as the Chief Rabbi maintains that the Scriptures referring to these circumstances are to be taken literally (*vide* Sermon IX., pp. 136-7), there will be no difficulty in proving that the lion, an

unclean beast of the forest, used in some passages of the
Scriptures as an emblem of untamed cruelty, has actually
eaten the same food as the ox, an animal used as a subject
of sacrifice, a beast of burden accustomed to the yoke, and
an emblem of obedience: they have both, with the leopard,
the kid, the calf, the young lion, the bear, and cow, all
fed together, and lain down in safety together, and a little
child, the little child that was born in Bethlehem of
Judæa, a Son that was given, has led them. The young
believer, who lives not by bread alone, but by every word
that proceedeth out of the *mouth* of Jehovah (Deut. viii. 3),
is made to dwell in safety, proof to the infidelity or
the poison of asps in the tongues of wicked and deceitful
men. If these things have not been so literally fulfilled,
then it remains for those who dispute it to prove that
Judah the son of Jacob was literally a lion's whelp, who
couched as a lion, and as an old lion; that Issachar was a
wild ass; that Dan was a serpent and an adder; that
Naphtali was a hind; that Joseph was a fruitful bough,
&c. Who can deny that the knowledge of the Lord is
spreading over the earth as the waters cover the sea? The
Bible is a spiritual pruning-hook, and a weapon that
ploughs up and exposes the depravity and the deceit of the
human heart, that has succeeded the sword, battle-axe,
and bayonet-point in religious debates and persecutions.

If Messiah has not come, where is the sceptre of Judah?
If Hezekiah was the child spoken of in Isaiah ix. 6, 7,
where are the evidences of the increase of his government
that was to have no end? If Messiah was an impostor,
how is it that His government continues to spread over the
earth? And how is it the Jews, instead of being established under the government of the throne of David, are a
scattered people, a bye-word and a proverb among the
nations? How is it that the Jews enjoy greater religious
liberty and temporal privileges under those governments
whose rulers are believers in the Nazarene as the Messiah
than under any other political administration? How is it
that the Prophets, whose writings testify of the Nazarene,
were treated with greater cruelty by the Jews than by
those who took the Jews captive (2 Chron. xxxvi. 16)?
Those questions are answered in Psalm cxviii. 22—"The
stone which the builders refused is become the head stone
of the corner." If the THREE letters composing the noun

D

אבן, *stone*, be examined, they will be found to express אב, Father, בן, Son. Reuchlin, an exponent of Kabbalah, proves that testimonies to the Messiah are to be deduced from the Hebrew by its doctrines: for instance, the letter ש, *shin*, is the symbol of fire or light, which, if inserted into the great and glorious name יהוה, Jehovah, expresses יהשוה, *Saviour*, the Hebrew equivalent for the Greek word Jesus (*vide* Ginsburg's Essay), called Messiah by Daniel, who can only be discerned by the inward persuasion and power of רוח אלהים, Spirit Ehlohim, revealed in the Scriptures as the third Eternal Person of the Godhead Ehlohim, the consideration of which I leave for a future publication (D.V.), wherein I hope to refute the other points of the sermons of the Chief Rabbi.

Since the vicarious atonement of Messiah there is no outward distinction *before God* between Jew or Gentile, bond or free, circumcision or uncircumcision, as will be seen: when the times of the Gentiles are fulfilled, God will remove the veil from the heart of the remnant of Israel He has sanctified to save under the new covenant. Messiah, called the Prince of Peace, told His disciples not to think He had come to send peace on earth, but a sword, because His kingdom was not of this world, as predicted throughout the Prophets. His very peace should cause Him to be despised and rejected of men (Isaiah liii.): "In those days and in that time, saith the Lord, the iniquity of Israel shall be sought for, and there shall be none; and the sins of Judah, and they shall not be found: for I will pardon them whom I reserve" (Jer. l. 20).

EDWARD POULSON.

FEBRUARY, 1870.

W. H. & L. Collingridge, Aldersgate Street, London, E.C.